A Good Friend

Other books in the Boys Town Teens and Relationships Series:

Vol. 2: Who's in the Mirror? Finding the Real Me

Vol. 3: What's Right for Me: Making Good Choices in Relationships

For a Boys Town Press catalog, call
1-800-282-6657

Teens who are having problems with relationships, drugs or alcohol use, depression, parental conflict, or any other kind of trouble, can call the Boys Town National Hotline, 1-800-448-3000, for help at any time.

A Good Friend

How to Make One, How to Be One

Ron Herron
Val J. Peter

BOYS
TOWN
PRESS

BOYS TOWN, NEBRASKA

A Good Friend

Published by The Boys Town Press
Father Flanagan's Boys' Home
Boys Town, Nebraska 68010

Publisher's Cataloging in Publication

(Prepared by Quality Books Inc.)

Herron, Ronald W.
　　Teens and relationships/by Ron Herron, Val J. Peter. –
1st ed.
　　p. cm.
　　LCCN:
　　ISBN: 1-889322-19-9 (v.1)
　　ISBN: 1-889322-20-2 (v.2)
　　ISBN: 1-889322-21-0 (v.3)
　　　CONTENTS: v. 1. A good friend: how to make one, how to
be one – v. 2. Who's in the mirror?: finding the real me – v.
3. What's right for me?: making good choices in
relationships.
　　　SUMMARY: Teaches teens skills to enable them to develop
self-esteem and healthy relationships with adults and other
young people.
　　　1. Teenagers–Conduct of life. 2. Interpersonal relations
in adolescence.　I. Peter, Val. J.　II. Father Flanagan's
Boys' Home.　III. Title.　IV. Title: Good friend　V. Title:
Who's in the mirror　VI. Title: What's right for me

BJ1661.H47 1998 　　　　　　158.1'0835
　　　　　　　　　　　　　　　QBI98–117

10　9　8　7　6　5　4　3　2　1

▼ Italicized quotes are excerpted from "Ginger Snaps," 1976, and "The Spice of Life," 1971, compiled by Dian Ritter, and published by C.R. Gibson, Norwalk, CT.

Book Credits

Editing: Terry Hyland
        Lynn Holm
        Lori Utecht
Production: Lisa Pelto
Cover Design: Brian Wilson
Page Layout: Michael Bourg

Table of Contents

Introduction

Relationships can be complex sometimes. They're confusing and tough to figure out. There are few easy answers about how to get along with others. And there are no guarantees that relationships will always be fun and rewarding. But learning how relationships develop will help you discover ways to make yours stronger and more satisfying.

This book is designed to help you improve all of your relationships. It is about getting along with adults, classmates, your family, and just about anyone with whom you come in contact. It's about making your current friendships better than they have ever been before. There are suggestions and tips for reaching your "relationship potential." That means letting others see the wonderful qualities you have and using those qualities to live a happier and more fulfilling life.

A Good Friend

Friendships and positive relationships can help make your life much better. They keep you moving in the right direction and help you cope with the problems you face. But dealing with all of the interwoven parts of relationships isn't easy. Your relationships will change with time; anything based on emotions and feelings usually does. This book gives you some simple, straightforward advice and encouragement that can help you.

And that's what friends are for.

The Basics of Friendship

Everyone needs friends. Friends are a principal source of happiness and hope in our lives. However, the ability to make friends varies from person to person. To some people, making friends is easy, and to others it's very difficult.

This chapter takes a look at what makes good friendships and talks about how you can learn to make new ones or make your current ones better. Good friends can help you become a better person. They help you know and understand yourself. Friendship is one of the most precious gifts you can give.

How does friendship start? Most people don't think a lot about it, but friendships don't just happen. There is an intriguing process that takes place between people. Let's start at the basics and look at relationships more closely.

! *A true friend is one who knows all about you and likes you just the same.*

Even though there are no rules or referees, no exact definitions or set formulas to human relationships, there are differences in the way we treat and feel about other people. We put people we know in three general categories: acquaintances, companions, and friends. What makes them different?

Acquaintances are people you see occasionally and perhaps say "hi" to or exchange small talk with. An acquaintance could be someone who rides the same bus as you, has a class with you, or works in the same place you do. Acquaintances also could include a bank teller who cashes your check, a waitress at your favorite restaurant, or a check-out clerk at a convenience store. Time spent around one another consists of brief encounters. You probably are pleasant to one another and get along okay, but there's not much more to it than that. Nothing has ever happened to make the relationship develop or change for better or worse; it's just there.

Companions, on the other hand, are closer to you because you share common experiences. You spend more time around these people than you do around acquaintances. You could be on the same sports team, share a locker at school, or be in a youth group together. You might work together, take the same classes in school, or live in the same neighborhood. The things you do together are tied to a common interest; it's kind of like the glue that holds your relationship together. You might have fun doing things together. It's also possible that you might not like each other that much, but you frequently find yourself doing the same things.

Friends are the "real deal." These are people you choose to spend a lot of time with. That's very different from the other two relationships.

Friends are special people because you do things for them as well as with them. Friends are there for the good times, bad times, and all the times in between. And having a "best friend" is wonderful.

Can these three relationships change? Of course they can. Sometimes a companion, or even an acquaintance, can become a friend. That's what makes friendship so exciting – just about anyone can become a friend.

Ten Rules for Friendship

Every person God put on this earth has a capacity to make friends – lots of friends. Unfortunately, most people never come close to reaching their "friendship potential." Making friends is a skill. And the first step in developing that skill is knowing how to get along with others. Friends don't become friends overnight. Friendships take time.

People who are good at getting along with others take an interest in what other people like. They learn to develop interests that make them enjoyable to be around. Therefore, the more things you know how to do that involve interacting with other people, the more likely you are to make friends.

If someone were to list the Ten Rules for Friendship, the following should be included:

✔ Do things together.
✔ Be honest.
✔ Talk about ideas, hopes and dreams, fears and disappointments.
✔ Encourage one another to do what's right.
✔ Be trustworthy and trusting.
✔ Talk out problems and disagreements.
✔ Look out for one another.
✔ Listen carefully to one another.
✔ Comfort each other in down times.
✔ Have fun.

That's it. If you can follow these rules, you don't need to read any further. Being a good friend will be simple.

❗ *Everybody has to be somebody to somebody to be anybody.*

But think for a minute. These rules aren't easy to live up to, are they? In fact, they are downright difficult. How many people do you know who treat others like that? Probably not many, or we wouldn't have all the problems we have today. We live in an imperfect world, and people have a habit of making others feel bad. So, before you put down this book, read a little more about what being a good friend is all about.

Let's look at Rule Number 10. It is listed last, but it may be the starting point for friendship. If you can have fun with someone, you set the stage for a deeper, more serious relationship to develop. It rarely happens in reverse. Having fun is a crucial element in friendship.

Having Fun Is No Joke

Having fun is healthy. It is a necessity; it keeps us emotionally fit, just as exercise keeps us physically fit. All people should relish the fact that they have the capacity to smile and laugh and feel good. And in the process, they can make others smile and laugh and feel good. That's pretty powerful. Other creatures can't enjoy life like we can; we're special.

Unfortunately, many people never reach their potential for having good, healthy fun with others. They shut other people out of their lives.

Some kids turn to video games or TV for fun and spend most of their time alone. There's nothing wrong with video games and TV. But they shouldn't take the place of people. Some kids take needless risks, such as using alcohol or other drugs, because they believe that fun can be found artificially. That's sad. The healthiest fun is right in front of them – friendships with other people.

Some adults have a problem making friends, too. There are some sour, angry grown-ups out there who never found out what it takes to get along with other people. They are lonely, bitter, and negative. The time for you to learn how to enjoy friends is now.

Try to put the following tips into practice. Then you will learn how to enjoy life and have fun with others.

1 Realize your own goodness. That's the beginning. All change comes from within you. You have skills and talents that others can enjoy. You really do. You also have a basic need to like others and be liked in return. Now is the time to meet that need.

You are worthy and good inside. Some people just don't let others see their true goodness; for whatever reasons, they keep it hidden. And when they do that, they cannot share themselves with others.

Once you begin to trust your own goodness, doubts and bad feelings are doomed. You'll still make mistakes; that's normal. But that doesn't make you a bad person. Once you feel good about yourself, you will be enjoyable to be around.

So, step number one: Realize and believe with all your heart that you are a good person who has something to share with others.

! *You grow up the day you have your first real laugh – at yourself.*

2 **Develop a sense of humor.** If you are always serious, lighten up. A scowl and a frown are "red lights" to friendship; they'll quickly stop people from approaching you. A smile and a laugh are "green lights" to friendship and show people how friendly you can be.

Learn to laugh at yourself and your shortcomings. It will relieve some of the stress in your life. If you ever feel like poking fun at someone, let it be you, never anyone else.

Look on the bright side. Look for humorous situations. Learn to tell jokes. There are lots of books, tapes, and movies that are genuinely funny; others are real groaners, but sometimes they make you laugh, too. Collect funny stories or comic strips. Learn how to make puns and have fun with language. Try to do some impersonations of famous people. And remember that tackling problems with a positive attitude takes care of needless worries.

There are times, of course, when laughing and joking around are not appropriate. Never let your sense of humor be disrespectful or rude. Laughter is good medicine, but it should be used at the right times.

Smile, smile, smile. It makes people wonder what you've been up to. It also is a friendly, open behavior.

❗ *No one was ever blinded by looking on the bright side of life.*

3 **Respect the rights of others.** They have their opinions; you have yours. Different opinions are healthy. Life would be pretty boring if everyone thought alike. Please don't think other people are stupid for disagreeing with you. Let them say what they think. And remember: You deserve the same respect from them.

Learn how to listen to others without putting them down or trying to convince them that your opinion is right. It's fun to look at things from another angle.

Six important words – "I admit I made a mistake."

Five important words – "You did a good job."

Four important words – "What do you think?"

Three important words – "Can I help?"

Two important words – "Thank you."

One important word – "We."

4 **Be kind**. This doesn't mean you are a wimp; it takes a great deal of courage. Throughout your life, you will learn that if you are kind to others, they probably will be kind to you. Kindness is one of the links in the chain that holds people together.

Being kind is like planting flower seeds that one day will bloom and be enjoyed. Being unkind is like planting weed seeds that grow up and choke out all the beauty around you. Don't help the weeds grow; we have enough unkindness already. Instead, scatter as many seeds of kindness as you can. And make sure you take the time to enjoy the flowers that grow from them.

When should you start being kind? Right now. Help someone in need. Give someone a compliment. Open the door for someone. Wave to a friend. Encourage someone who is down.

Say something positive. There are hundreds of little things you can do to show kindness.

You'll find that being kind is a profitable investment, one that pays big dividends. Not only will other people like you, but you'll also like yourself and feel good inside. That's the best of both worlds.

! *It's nice to be important – but much more important to be nice.*

5 **Be empathetic.** In other words, try to understand what others are going through. Look at life through their eyes. Remember times when you felt the same way, and remember how much it hurt. If you empathize and understand someone's feelings, you can help.

Friendships are fragile and require as much care in handling as other fragile and precious things.

6 **Don't complain.** People get tired of listening to constant whining. It accomplishes nothing except turning other people off. Life doesn't always go the way you want. Learn to accept what you can't change, and work hard to change what you can. Forget about the little things that bug you. Replace the time you used to spend complaining with time spent being kind.

7 **Don't stop being friendly.** Even if you are faced with negative, closed-minded people, never give up. Don't let them change you into one of them. Continue to be kind and friendly. Show them your goodness, and things will usually be okay.

Following these tips will help you have fun. You see, having fun isn't just laughing, playing, and joking around, although they are important. Having fun also means having a sense of enjoyment and pleasure.

Let's look at when and where you can put these ideas to use.

Meeting People and Making Friends

Getting along with others requires action. You can't sit back and hope that friends will fall from the sky. You have to get out and meet people. If you're shy, see the last chapter for tips.

The first step is simple. Go places that you enjoy, and do things that you like to do. In the process, you will meet others who enjoy similar interests. Having something in common means you will have more to talk about. Pick a time to "break the ice" with someone. Make it light and casual, like, "Do you come here a lot?" or "You're good at that." Improve your conversation skills.

The next chapter contains many tips about improving your ability to talk with others.

It doesn't matter what your interests are. What is important is doing something that will help you meet other people. If you don't have a lot of interests that involve being with others, get busy. Find things that you're good at, and learn how to use them to meet other people. Get to know other kids by being involved in sports, music, clubs, church groups, and other extracurricular activities. It makes sense that the more people you meet and talk with, the more likely you are to find people who have the qualities you look for in a friend.

Keep reading. The next chapters contain other suggestions that will help you meet people and make friends.

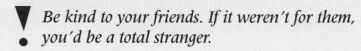

Be kind to your friends. If it weren't for them, you'd be a total stranger.

Conversation Building Blocks

Building positive relationships is like building a house. First, there has to be a sturdy foundation. One of the building blocks used in the foundation of good relationships is conversation.

Knowing how to talk casually and comfortably is important if you want to meet and get along with other people. Unfortunately, not everyone is good at it. No one hops out of the baby crib with the ability to talk to other people. The "gift of gab" is a learned skill.

It's easy to talk with close friends, but many struggle when it comes to talking with people they don't know very well. Bashful people want to avoid meeting others altogether. They tell themselves it isn't worth the hassle. What they're really doing is covering the fact that they are afraid of feeling awkward and looking foolish. That's understandable, but it can be overcome with some effort.

Being good at conversation is no different than being good at spelling, sports, or video games. Some people may have more natural talent than others, but all skills, including conversation, can be learned if you're willing to work at them. You just have to know what to do, and then practice. Successful athletes, musicians, carpenters, mechanics, and business executives all become experts by practicing their skills over and over. The same is true with conversation skills. The more you use them, the better you get.

If you want to get anywhere in this world, a lot is going to hinge on how well you can talk with others. Most jobs involve meeting people and exchanging conversation or at least making friendly small talk. So, unless you want to live in a tent in the middle of the woods, take the time to learn conversation skills. If you've ever backed away from meeting or talking to someone, now is the time to learn some basic behaviors that will help you in many places – at home, at school, on the job, with new people, at interviews, with friends, and in countless other situations.

⊦ Ray's Story

Ray is a kid who has trouble making friends. When he comes into a room, he doesn't wait to see what's going on, but jumps right into the conver-

sation. He interrupts when others are talking, and then monopolizes the conversation. He brags about his accomplishments and exaggerates or tells lies to the other kids. He has told them that his dad gets tickets every year to the Super Bowl, and that his family has a vacation home in Hawaii, but the kids know that isn't true. He wants to have friends; in fact, his bragging and lies are told to impress the other kids and make them like him. But Ray doesn't realize that he is actually driving the other kids away. Ray needs to learn better conversation skills that show the others that he is trustworthy and is both an interesting person to be around and interested in what they have to say.

Getting Started

Let's start at the beginning – first impressions. You probably have felt nervous upon meeting someone, especially if you wanted to make a good first impression. This person could have been a teacher, a boss, a coach, someone you wanted to date, a police officer – just about anyone who could have had some effect on your life. The pressure's on, and it can be nerve-wracking.

▼ *You never get a second chance to make a good*
● *first impression.*

17

Here's what happens with first impressions: When people first meet you, they form a mental picture of you and store it for later recall, just as a computer would recall a saved message. What they recall is very important to how they may treat you later. After meeting you, it would be nice if they thought, "Wow! What a nice person! I was impressed." Having someone remember good things about you can open the door to many opportunities.

What prevents people from making a good impression on others? In some situations, people get the jitters – clammy hands, a dry tongue and throat, forgetfulness. If you've ever experienced these symptoms, you know how unpleasant they are. It's easier just to clam up and clear out. There's probably not an adult alive who has forgotten how nervous he or she was on a first date!

Whenever you meet someone new, it's a good idea to have a greeting statement in mind. Usually, just saying "hello" and telling the person your name works fine. It's also important to pay careful attention to what the other person does and says. This will help you decide what you are going to do in response. Not saying anything, mumbling, or being nervous are sure turn-offs.

Conversation Skills

Talking with others is like playing a game of catch. When you play catch, one person begins by tossing the ball to someone, and that person throws it back. It's simple, an equal arrangement.

Let's say you throw the ball to someone, and it's not thrown back. Maybe that person keeps it, throws it to someone else, or ignores you altogether. What happens? You feel left out, hurt, or puzzled. You're no longer a part of the game. You can feel just as "out of the game" when people don't "play catch" with you in conversation.

Conversation is an interactive skill. One person plays off what the other says. If people know the rules of the game, everyone has a good time and gets a chance to play.

The following tips can help you improve your conversation skills:

1 **Look at the person you're talking to.** This simple behavior is tremendously important. The best way to begin any interaction is to make eye contact.

Looking at a person shows that you are confident, interested, and paying attention. You're also much more likely to understand what the other person is saying. And people tend to trust someone who has the confidence to look them straight in the eye. That's a big benefit for such a simple behavior, isn't it?

Just make sure that you don't stare, squint, or wear a negative expression. Try to look at the person as you would look at a friend, and you'll have fewer problems.

! *Of all the things you wear, your expression is the most important.*

2 Be relaxed when you talk with others – or at least look relaxed. There are many behaviors that indicate that you're nervous or tense. Be sure you don't look away or down at the floor, stare at your hands, fidget, bite your nails, yawn, or shuffle your feet. People might think that you're being rude or disrespectful, that you're not paying attention, or that you just don't care. Instead, nod your head, smile (if appropriate), or say something to show that you're listening. If you're nervous, take a deep breath before you begin talking. More than anything else, a pleasant facial expression shows other people that you are confident and at ease.

3 Don't interrupt or monopolize a conversation. Even if you're bursting to say something, wait until the other person has finished talking. If you're speaking, encourage the other person to share his opinion by asking, "What do you think?" This politely encourages more conversation. People like to be included in a conversation, and no one likes to talk to a "know-it-all."

> ❗ *It's all right to hold a conversation, but you have to let go of it every now and then.*

4 Ask questions. Many conversations begin with one person asking another a question. You are with plenty of kids each day who are likely candidates for a conversation with you. Go for it. People give off signals that indicate openness. Look for someone who seems friendly and happy. Don't pick the loudest person or one who makes fun of other kids.

Learn to ask questions that require more than a "yes" or "no" response. If you have had trouble coming up with questions in the past because you were nervous, think of some possibilities beforehand. Ask for someone's opinion. Opinions give you some idea of what a person is all about. But if you ask for an opinion, make sure you really want to hear it. You will appear much more interested if you really are interested! Be aware of what's happening at school, and ask others what they think. Ask about a person's favorite foods, sports, or hobbies. For example, you can ask, "What's your favorite place to eat?" or "What's your favorite TV show?"

Keep your questions general and easy to answer. You're not looking for someone to marry or the key to world peace; you just want to start a conversation. Always make sure not to ask questions that are too personal. Otherwise, you run the risk of making enemies instead of friends.

If someone asks you to mind your own business, say you're sorry, and walk away. Don't try to explain yourself. Maybe you picked the wrong time or the wrong person. For example, when a group of friends you don't know are together, laughing and joking around, it's probably not a good idea to try to join in. They may think you're trying to "butt in" on their conversation. It's usually better to begin a conversation with one person, rather than an established group.

Usually, however, showing interest by asking questions is a good way to begin a conversation. Don't go out looking for a best friend; your only goal is to get better at talking with others. People will share more about themselves if they are comfortable talking with you, and it's possible that a close relationship will develop. But early on, conversation should be light and casual.

5 Use your voice to your advantage. The way you say something is very important.

You send signals with your voice. That means you can sound interested, concerned, sympathetic, dynamic, enthusiastic, upset, silly, and so on, just by the way you say something. Vary your voice to fit the impression you want others to have of you.

Make sure the volume of your voice fits the situation. Yelling is fine at a ball game, but don't do it in church. A whisper is good sometimes, but at other times it indicates a lack of confidence. And you probably know how aggravating it is when you go to a movie theater and someone talks or laughs so others can't hear the movie. Always judge the situation; then talk with the correct volume level.

Along with volume, consider your voice inflection. That means you stress certain words, or say them in a way that mirrors what you are feeling. A good example is a sports announcer who is reporting an exciting play. The announcer relays the drama with vivid language and skillful use of inflection. His or her voice goes up and down, speaking fast then slowly, loudly then softly, all the while emphasizing certain words that give the audience a crystal-clear image of what is happening. The way the action is described makes you want to pay attention.

On the other hand, think of someone who speaks in a dull, droning monotone. It's hard to stay awake, right? The next thing you know, you're daydreaming, and you've completely missed what the person said.

If you don't know what your voice sounds like, talk into a tape recorder. You may be surprised by what you hear. Most people's reaction is "That's not me! I don't sound like that!" Have some fun with it. Try to imitate other people or talk with an accent. Sing a song, or read from a book. You can find many different ways to say the same words.

Practice varying your voice volume and inflection. Here's an experiment: Say the following sentences out loud and emphasize the word in bold print each time. Really stress the word. Be dramatic. You may be surprised by how the meaning of the sentence changes.

I did not say he stole the money.

I **did** not say he stole the money.

I did **not** say he stole the money.

I did not **say** he stole the money.

I did not say **he** stole the money.

I did not say he **stole** the money.

I did not say he stole **the** money.

I did not say he stole the **money.**

See how the meaning changes? Volume and inflection can change the message you give other people. Even a simple "okay" can show excitement, boredom, or anger, depending on the way you say it.

Just a word of caution: Don't go overboard. When you're talking with people, don't pretend you're auditioning for a part in a play. They will think you're goofy if you overdo it. But you can learn to use inflection to get your message across. That's using your voice to your advantage.

6 **Look for people who have the same interests and values as you.** It's easier to talk to someone who likes the things you like.

> *A gossip is one who talks to you about others.*
> *A bore is one who talks only about himself.*
> *A brilliant conversationalist is one who talks to you about yourself.*

7 **Start by talking about the other person's interests.** Once you get people talking about themselves – their hobbies, goals, or interests – it's easy to keep the conversation going by asking more questions. People like to talk about their interests. Listen attentively. People are usually impressed when you remember what they said earlier.

8 **Have a wide variety of subjects to talk about.** Keep up with what's happening; know what's going on in school and in your neighborhood. Read about sports, current events, music, and movies. Not having anything to add to a conversation can make you feel left out and foolish. You don't have to be an expert, but you should know enough to be able to come up with some intelligent questions.

If you don't know much about a certain topic, ask someone who does. Let the person talk. He'll probably feel good about knowing so much, and you may learn something new in the process. That will give you something to talk about later.

! *If it had been intended for humans to talk twice as much as listen, they would have been given two mouths and one ear.*

9 **Pay attention.** Carefully listen to and watch what the other person says and does. This may sound simple, but many people don't pay attention very well. You can find out a lot about another person by carefully listening to his or her choice of words and voice inflection and by watching facial expressions and body language. These signs can give you clues about whether a person is sincere, friendly, or kind, and also may indicate whether they are interested in what you have to say. If a person yawns, looks at his watch, or says "huh?" frequently while you're talking, he's either tired or bored. Missing or misreading these types of cues can be embarrassing.

It's much better to talk with someone who helps keep the conversation going by saying, "Wow, that's great!" or "You're kidding!" or "What happened next?" Those comments make a person feel good about sharing information with someone.

So remember: What a person says and does can help you decide whether to continue on with the same topic, talk about something else, or end the conversation.

10 **Express your feelings and opinions.** Many of the previous suggestions will help you to get others talking and sharing. But if your goal is to develop relationships by using your conversation skills, you also have to share your thoughts and feelings. Let people look into your life, but disclose only what you want them to know about you. Don't share personal thoughts when you are just beginning to know someone.

Be honest. Some people tend to brag or create a false impression of themselves in the hope that other people will like them. This isn't effective and rarely leads to a close relationship. Tell it like it is, and you'll be okay. It's all right to share your weaknesses as well as your strengths. People view you as open and "human" when you can admit mistakes or laugh at your shortcomings. But be sure to balance how much you talk about your successes and your failures. Talking too much about what you do right might make you come across as self-centered; talking too much about what you do wrong might make you appear to be a loser. Remember: What you say gives people an impression of you as a total person. Give them an accurate picture.

11 **Keep trying.** Once you decide you're ready to begin a conversation with someone, go ahead. Just remember three basic guidelines: Be simple and direct; be honest; be enthusiastic. These are crucial keys to making a good first impression and having a good conversation. If you make a couple of mistakes along the way, like saying the wrong thing, don't worry about it. There's an old saying that goes, "If at first you don't succeed, try, try again." It might be just as accurate to say, "If at first you don't succeed, you're running about average!" Everyone makes mistakes; learn from yours, and keep going.

These tips aren't meant to make you a brilliant conversationalist. But they can help you feel more relaxed and at ease when you talk with other people. If you're really serious about wanting to improve your conversation skills, all it takes is a little work. You may have to practice what to say and how to say it, and learn to pay closer attention to the reactions of others. But if you do, you will find it easier than ever before to carry on meaningful, funny, or exciting conversations. People will want to be around you if you are friendly and pleasant and have something interesting to say.

▼
● *If you see someone without a smile, share one of yours.*

In summary, here are some ways to start a conversation, keep it going, and then end it:

Starting a Conversation

✔ Ask for the other person's opinion.
✔ Give a compliment.
✔ Ask for help.
✔ Give your opinion.

Keeping the Conversation Going

✔ Express interest in what the other person says.
✔ Ask follow-up questions.

✔ Offer your opinion.
✔ Change the topic if necessary.
✔ Ask personal (but not too personal) questions.

Ending the Conversation

✔ Stop talking about a topic if nothing interesting comes to mind.
✔ Express appreciation for the other person's thoughts and move on.
✔ Always end on a positive note by using one or more of the following:

> Giving compliments – "Thanks a lot. You really helped me."
>
> Showing appreciation – "It's been nice talking with you."
>
> Showing interest in seeing the person in the future – "Maybe we can talk again sometime."
>
> Making an ending statement – "I've got to get to class now. See you later."

Getting Along
with Others

Getting along with others sounds simple. It isn't. Human beings are complex, and some are hard to figure out. All people have unique personalities, different ways of looking at things, and different sets of circumstances that make them who they are. Some people make it easy for others to get to know and like them, and others make it very difficult.

Why is it so important to learn to get along with others? A great deal of the enjoyment or pain you experience in your life will depend on how successful you are in dealing with other people. This includes not only acquaintances, companions, and friends as we talked about in the first chapter but also includes strangers.

If you have positive interactions, life will go much more smoothly for you. The opposite also is true. If you can't get along with others, life will be a lot more difficult.

Getting along with others doesn't mean being phony or purposely "kissing up." That behavior is practiced by selfish manipulators, who only want something in return. Sooner or later, people see through this kind of behavior and realize how insincere or sneaky a person like this is.

Getting along with others means doing things because you care about others and respect their rights and opinions. In a nutshell, getting along with others means you treat others the way you want to be treated. That's not being phony; that's simply being a good person.

Let's look on the other side of the coin. When people don't get along with one another, the result is hassles, arguments, bad feelings, fights, and a lot of tension. Nothing constructive.

! *It's funny that people will try so hard to look good – and try so little to be good.*

It may not be possible to get along with everyone. There are people who are rude, crude, aggressive, antisocial, or just plain negative. You shouldn't spend your life trying to change them or to strike up friendships with them. You probably can't avoid them, and you don't have to like them, but it's in your best interest to at least know how to get along with them. If you show some respect and courtesy to them, they might treat you a little bit better in return.

▐ LaShawn's Story

LaShawn is unhappy much of the time. His teachers send frequent reports home to his parents about problems he's having with teachers, administrators, and, especially, his peers. LaShawn doesn't seem to know how to get along with others. He is uncooperative, often refusing to help with group projects. When walking in the halls, he will often bump into other students, and he usually yells at them, even though it was his fault. Lately, he's been getting into fights after school. Other kids who have seen what's going on say it is almost always LaShawn's fault. Believe it or not, LaShawn says that he wants other kids to like him, and that he doesn't like always being in trouble. His parents are worried about LaShawn's behavior and have met with the school counselor to see if they can't help LaShawn get along better with others. He's listening to what they have to say, and trying to change.

Attention!

Getting along with others hinges on your ability to give positive attention to people. When you are attentive, you can figure out how to make the best of each situation. Using behaviors that other people like and accept increases the chance that you will "fit in" with a wide variety of people.

Look around you. Watch the other kids in school. It will become clear that there are three basic ways you can behave toward other people: You can avoid them, give them negative attention, or give them positive attention. You see these behaviors in action everyday, in all kinds of situations.

How do people avoid others? They ignore them. They don't talk to or look at them. They don't listen or respond to them. People also can avoid situations where they would have to be with other people: a dance, a party, or some other get-together. You can't give people attention if you're not around them. That also means you will never learn to get along with them.

Then there's negative attention. You might see someone making fun of another kid, saying mean things, starting rumors, picking fights, arguing, or making faces. These are definite ways to give other people negative attention.

Teenagers know how to give adults negative attention – sighing, rolling their eyes, shrugging their shoulders, making a sarcastic or rude comment, refusing to follow instructions. These behaviors are obvious signs of disrespect and dislike, and they don't help you get along with adults.

Giving someone negative attention usually results in more problems. One person's feelings are hurt, that person does something to retaliate, and the whole vicious cycle continues. It's hard to understand why people choose to live in such turmoil, always at odds with someone else.

What about giving positive attention? This makes other people feel good and worthwhile. It certainly takes no more effort than doing all those nasty, negative things. And doing positive things creates positive feelings, for you as well as for the person you're dealing with. When people try to get along with each other, there is a sense of calm and cooperation, not the tension that results when people don't care about others.

Behaviors That Help You Get Along with Others

There are some very basic behaviors that will help you get along with other people – adults as well as kids your age:

1 **Give compliments to the other person.** When people take the time to notice the good things other people do, it creates a friendly, cooperative atmosphere. And it's so simple to do!

Make your praise short and to the point. Don't ramble on and on; it sounds phony and becomes annoying. Just tell the person what you like, and leave it at that.

Most people like hearing someone say something nice about them. They will consider you a nice person for noticing.

! *Nothing improves a person's hearing more than praise.*

2 Accept compliments. Don't make someone feel bad about saying something nice to you. It's a real turn-off to give someone a compliment and then have the person say, "Oh, I really didn't do as well as I could have." It's almost like the person is disagreeing with you. It's a quick way to stop getting compliments!

All you have to do is tell the person that you appreciate him or her taking the time to notice, or return the compliment: "You did a nice job, too." If you can't think of anything else, a good old-fashioned "thanks" will work just fine.

3 Be pleasant. Greet people in a friendly way: say "hi;" call them by their first names; wave at them; nod your head when you agree; use a pleasant voice; smile. Answer questions right away; volunteer to help; follow up on a previous conversation. And just like you learned when you were little, say the magic words "please" and "thank you."

Good manners and politeness aren't out-of-style. Even though it may seem as though some people want to put them on the endangered species list, you can help them make a strong comeback. Pleasantness is contagious and will catch on if you give it a chance.

4 **Comfort others.** One way to do this is to offer empathy. That means being sensitive to what someone is going through. There will be other times when you can offer sympathy. That means you feel sorry for someone and want to help in times of sadness or disappointment. This could be a person who is struggling in school or another activity, a classmate whose family is in crisis, or a friend who is trying to cope with the death of someone close. Sympathy and empathy offer a little light at a dark time in people's lives.

5 **Let little irritations "roll off your back."** Some people let small things ruin their whole day. They get cranky or worried every time something doesn't go their way. Then they take their frustrations out on others. If you have a classmate, boss, or friend who gets upset easily, you know how uncomfortable being around that person can be.

Don't sweat the small stuff. Life is full of minor irritations, and, just like mosquitoes, they frustrate and annoy us. But there are ways to get rid of mosquitoes; use a repellent, and they don't bother you anymore. A positive attitude can be enough to repel the things that bug you.

Learn to keep your focus and poise. Keep moving ahead with the task at hand, and put the little irritations out of your mind. If you can change some of the things that annoy you, great. Go for it. But spending time worrying about things that really don't make a big difference in your life is a waste of time. Forget the little pests that used to make you mad. Keep your cool, and things will usually work out for the better.

6 **Don't hold grudges.** Learn how to forgive and forget. Don't try to get even with someone who hurt or offended you. Don't complain that whatever happened to you was someone else's fault. Spend your time doing something good with your life. Learn from what happened, and keep moving ahead.

7 **Reward only positive behavior.** Don't pay attention to people who are displaying negative behavior. Instead, give compliments and positive attention for positive behavior.

! *If you were someone else, would you want to be friends with you?*

8 **Concentrate on what is going right, instead of what is going wrong.** When you talk to other people, bring up the positive things that are happening around you. Many people focus on the negative things in life. There are many, to be sure, but why attach more importance to them than they deserve? Focus on what is going right, and you allow other people to focus on positive things as well.

9 **Learn to be less critical.** Encourage those around you. Build them up. Even though it is usually easy to see faults in others, ignore what you can. There are reasons people behave the way they do. Don't condemn or criticize. Instead, be more flexible and accepting of them. In so doing, you will become kind and forgiving.

10 **Be a good listener.** Listening to others is a positive way to communicate. Too many people think the world revolves around them, and they don't take time to listen or understand others. Listening carefully shows your openness and concern for other people. They will appreciate your attention.

All of these behaviors can help you get along with others. Remember to do these things enthusiastically, sincerely, and frequently, and you will find your relationships with others rewarding and positive.

People Skills

Most people have general impressions of others. They may view someone as friendly, nice, stuck-up, or immature. The odds are that a "friendly" person knows how to use social skills that are acceptable and pleasing to other people and an "unfriendly" person does not.

Social skills, or "people skills," are sets of behaviors – usually simple things – that help us get along with others. When you put these behaviors together in a certain order, they make up a skill. A person who has good social skills is more likely to develop positive relationships. In turn, people who have positive relationships are more likely to be successful in whatever they do.

You need social skills both to get along with others and to get along in life. They really are "survival skills." Many things that happen to you depend on how well you handle social situations, so make a serious effort to improve.

How can you improve your social skills? First, you must take action. You can't sit back and expect good things to happen to you. Chances are they won't. You can be the nicest human being on earth, but it won't make much difference unless other people get to know you.

Second, you have to believe that you can achieve your goals. That takes confidence. That means learning and practicing social skills before you need to use them.

Finally, you have to go out and use the skills you learn. Use them every day. You will be pleasantly surprised by how much happier you are and how much control you have over your life.

Although social skills can be used in many different situations, you have to know how to use each one. Sometimes adjustments are needed. Take greeting skills, for instance. The way you greet a friend is different from the way you greet a teacher (at least it should be). Both greetings should be pleasant and friendly, but you should be more formal toward your teacher. It's the same as a good mechanic knowing which tool to use to fix a car. Knowing which skill to use and how, when, and where to use it makes a big difference in the impression you make on other people.

Why Use Social Skills?

Most of us want approval and acceptance from others. We feel left out and rejected if we don't fit in. If a person doesn't have the social skills to handle a certain situation, it's easy for him or her to withdraw from others or let negative emotions build. It makes some people shy, lonely, depressed, or angry at the whole world.

On the other hand, knowing how to use social skills correctly will change your life for the better. A wide range of social skills helps you know what to do or say in a given situation, even when the situation is negative.

▌ Devon's Story

Devon was driving home from school a few weeks ago when she spotted flashing lights behind her. She soon realized it was a state patrol vehicle, but she assumed he was going after someone ahead of her on the road and kept driving. Finally, the patrolman pulled up in the lane next to her and motioned her to pull over. She was upset; she knew she hadn't been speeding, so she assumed that the officer was just trying to harass her because she was a teenager. She pulled over and began rummaging in the glove compartment for her registration slip. The patrolman tapped on her window and asked if she would please pull her hand away from the glove box and get out of the car. Devon jumped out of the car and snapped at the patrolman, "Don't you have better things to do than harass people who aren't doing anything wrong? Surely there's some criminal somewhere who needs to be arrested!" Devon wouldn't listen to what the patrolman had to say, and she continued complaining and arguing with him. As you've probably guessed, Devon's response only made things worse. The officer had just pulled her over because she had a taillight out, but because of her behavior, Devon received a ticket with several violations and citations listed, and found herself facing a court date and a heavy fine.

What Devon needed were some social skills. A police officer expects certain behaviors, especially showing respect. Devon also needed to know how to follow instructions. That's one of the most important social skills of all.

What should she have done? Someone stopped by a police officer shouldn't reach for anything until told by the officer exactly what to do. Devon shouldn't have made sudden movements, and she should not have given excuses. She should have used a calm voice, answered "yes" or "no" instead of using a flippant response, and slowly taken out her license and registration when the officer asked for them. Many teens who get stopped by the police make the situation worse, either because they don't know what to do, or because they refuse to follow instructions.

Complaining, sighing loudly, or acting disrespectful is an open invitation for more trouble whenever you are dealing with any person who has some form of authority over you – a boss, teacher, police officer, or judge. This is true for adults as well as teenagers; grown-ups can be poor role models at times. Many people think that they can push their way through life doing things "their way." It doesn't work like that most of the time, and it's a painful lesson to learn. If someone in authority is abusing his or her power, that's a different situation altogether. Get someone you trust to help you then.

In most cases, knowing how to follow instructions is an important skill that will probably result in the best outcome (or fewest negative consequences) for you.

Do Your Homework

Most of us don't know what to do when we're faced with a new situation—such as answering a police officer's questions, applying for a job, or meeting a date's parents. That makes sense, doesn't it? Usually, we just have to guess and hope things work out. That isn't always the most pleasant way to learn. You're going to make some painful mistakes if you don't learn some skills to cope with the problems littered along life's highway. Therefore, it's important to think ahead. If you don't know how to respond in a certain situation, ask your mom or dad, or an older friend or relative you trust. It's very important to ask questions. Think things through logically before you are placed in the real situation. Practice as if you were actually facing it.

If you think someone you know has good social skills, observe what he or she says and does that others find appealing. You can learn from the positive examples other people set for you. Figure out how you can use those skills and how they will help you.

Think of situations your friends didn't handle well. Learn from their mistakes. Know what you're going to do and how you're going to do it. You don't have to be caught unaware.

You're going to experience many new situations as you grow up. If the only way you learn is by getting a negative consequence, you're learning the hard way. You can avoid many problems by learning social skills. Do yourself a favor by thinking ahead.

Getting Started

While there are many social skills, ranging from simple to complex, there are a few that you will use almost every day. By studying and practicing these skills, you will be better prepared to handle many daily social interactions and will learn how to adjust them to fit other situations.

Begin by developing a social skills training program. Here are some things to think about:

✔ Pick one skill you want to improve. Let's say you want to improve your ability to give compliments. Make a goal for yourself, such as, "I will give compliments to three people today." Make sure you're able to accomplish the goal; then do it.

✔ Chart your progress. Some people use a daily journal to keep track of their goals, and note successes or problems along the way. You could make a chart and use stick-on stars to show when you have accomplished part or all of your goal. The main thing is to have a visual way to show you are improving. Don't leave it to memory.

✔ Praise yourself when you reach a goal. Tell yourself, "I really did a good job," or "I'm pleased at how hard I tried." Treat yourself to something special when you meet one of your goals.

Nine Necessary Social Skills

The following nine skills are the ones you probably will use often. Master each of them. The more you use them, the more they will become like second nature to you. Each skill is divided into steps; some hints on how to do each step are included. Go get 'em!

Following Instructions

1 **Look at the person.** This will show that you are paying attention and will help you understand his or her mood. Avoid being distracted. Look at the person as you would a friend. Don't stare, make faces, or roll your eyes.

2 **Say "okay."** This lets the person know that you understand. Answer right away. Speak clearly, using a pleasant tone of voice, and then smile and nod your head (if it is appropriate to do so).

3 **Do the task immediately.** You are more likely to remember exactly what you're supposed to do if you do it right away. Complete each step of the task. Stay on task, and do the best job you can. If you have problems, ask for help.

4 **Check back.** This lets the person know that you have followed the instructions. Tell the person as soon as you have finished. Explain exactly what you did, and ask if the job was done properly. Correct anything that's incorrect.

Accepting "No"

1 **Look at the person to show that you are paying attention.** This will also help you understand what the other person is saying. Don't stare, make faces, or look away. If you are upset, control your emotions. Try to relax and stay calm.

2 **Say "okay."** This lets the other person know that you understand. Answer right away in a clear voice. Don't mumble, sound angry, or start to argue. That might lead to more problems. Take a deep breath if you feel upset.

3 **Calmly ask for a reason if you really don't understand.** People will think you are serious about wanting to know a reason if you ask for one calmly. Don't keep asking for more reasons after you receive one. Don't ask for a reason every time, or you will be viewed as a complainer.

4 **If you disagree, bring it up later.** If you disagree right away, you will appear to be arguing. Take some time to plan how you are going to approach the person who told you "no" and what you are going to say. Accept the answer, even if it is still "no." Be sure to thank the person for listening.

Giving Compliments

1 Look at the person and smile. This starts the interaction on a positive note.

2 Speak with a clear, enthusiastic voice. Your enthusiasm adds "spice" to what you say. A compliment loses its zip if you act as if you don't mean it.

3 Tell the person exactly what you liked. Being specific will make you feel more confident and less likely to fumble for words. Noticing what another person did well will make you appear like a friendly and caring individual.

4 Don't overdo it. Keep the compliment short.

5 Give the person time to respond to your compliment. Don't rush into another topic. Sometimes people don't know what to say, so don't expect them to respond immediately.

116954

Accepting Compliments

1 **Look at the person.** This shows that you are interested in what he or she has to say, and it will make him or her feel more comfortable talking to you.

2 **Don't shuffle your feet or act embarrassed.** If you are uneasy, the other person will be, too. Take a deep breath if you are nervous.

3 **Use a pleasant voice.** This will show friendliness and openness.

4 **Thank the person.** Don't waste a lot of time wondering why someone gave you a compliment; just appreciate the fact that someone took the time to say something nice to you. There are several ways to thank a person. Show appreciation: "Thanks a lot" or "Thanks for noticing." Return the compliment: "You did a great job, too." Agree: "I was happy with the way it turned out. I worked hard on it." (But don't overdo this one. It could sound like bragging if you said, "Yeah. I was awesome, wasn't I!")

Introducing Yourself

1 **Look at the person and smile.** This sets a friendly tone for the beginning of your conversation and is one way of showing that you really want to meet him or her. Get the person's attention appropriately. Don't stare or make faces; rather, look at the person as you would a friend.

2 **Use a pleasant voice.** You will make a good impression if you appear friendly. Speak clearly and loudly enough to be heard, but don't yell. Use proper grammar, and avoid slang words.

3 **State your name.** People need to know who you are. Wait for the right time to introduce yourself and say your name as if you were proud of it. Share other information about yourself, if appropriate. Listen when the other person states his or her name.

4 **Shake the person's hand.** This is a traditional way of greeting someone. Use a firm grip, but don't squeeze too hard. Three shakes are about right when shaking hands. Say, "It's nice to meet you," as you shake hands. Make sure your hand is clean before shaking hands with someone. (If your hand is dirty and it's not appropriate to leave, say, "Excuse me," and briefly explain the situation.)

5 **When departing, again say, "It was nice to meet you."** Saying good-bye ends your conversation on a friendly note. Shake the person's hand again, if appropriate, when you leave, and use his or her name when saying good-bye. Remember their name in case you meet again.

Disagreeing Appropriately

1 **Look at the person throughout your conversation to show that you are paying attention.** Don't stare or make faces. Have a pleasant facial expression, and look at the person as you would a friend.

2 **Use a pleasant voice.** The person is more likely to listen to you. Speak slowly, clearly, and use short sentences, which are more easily understood. Keep a comfortable distance between you and the other person while you are talking. Smile: People are more comfortable talking with someone who is friendly.

3 **Make a sincere empathy/concern statement.** A statement like "I know this was a difficult job" or "I know you're upset by this" gets the conversation off to a positive start. Plan what you are going to say before you start to speak. If you still feel uneasy about how you are going to start your conversation, practice. Discuss your concerns as part of a conversation, not a confrontation. Be sincere.

4 **Be specific when telling why you disagree.** Using vague words can be confusing and doesn't get your point across. Use as much detailed information as possible, and be prepared to back up what you say. If necessary, practice what you are going to say. Always remember to think before you speak.

5 **Give a reason.** Your disagreement will carry more weight if you give a valid reason. Be sure that your reasons (one or two are usually enough) make sense. Support your reasons with facts and details, if necessary. Remember to stay calm during the conversation.

6 **Say, "thank you."** This shows that you appreciate the person's taking the time to listen to you. Remember to say "thank you," even if you didn't get the response you wanted. Being polite makes it more likely that the person will listen to you in the future and ends the conversation on a positive note.

Showing Respect

1 **Obey a request to stop a negative behavior.** This shows that you can follow instructions and may also help you avoid getting into trouble. There will always be people who have authority over you. It shows respect to do what they say.

2 **Refrain from teasing, threatening, or making fun of others.** This shows you understand that these behaviors can hurt the feelings of others. If you make fun of or threaten people, you won't have many friends.

3 **Allow others their privacy.** Sometimes people need or want to be alone. Always knock before entering someone's room or a room with a closed door.

4 **Obtain permission before using another person's property.** You have certain possessions that are very important to you, and you don't want people using them without permission. When you ask permission to use others' things, you show that same kind of respect. Always return items in the same condition as when you borrowed them. If you do damage a borrowed item, offer to repair or replace it.

5 **Do not damage or vandalize public property.** Vandalizing and damaging property are against the law. Besides getting into trouble, you show disrespect for your community when you vandalize public property. Accidents do happen, but they always should be reported. Offer to replace or repair property you have damaged.

6 **Don't persuade others to break rules.** People will think less of you if you are always trying to take advantage of others or get them into trouble. If you use people, they won't trust you.

7 **Avoid acting obnoxious in public.** You make a good impression with people when you show that you know how to behave and use proper social skills in public. Be on your best behavior. That means don't do such things as curse, swear, spit, and belch.

8 **Dress appropriately.** People are expected to look their best in public. When you live up to this expectation, you show that you are mature and understand society's rules. Being well-groomed and well-dressed makes a good impression. Use good judgment when deciding what to wear, letting the occasion dictate your choice of dress.

Showing Sensitivity to Others

1 **Express interest in and concern for others, especially when they are having trouble.** If you help others, they are more likely to help you. If you see someone in trouble, ask if you can help. Sometimes just showing you care is enough to help a person get through a difficult time.

2 **Recognize that disabled people deserve the same respect as anyone else.** A physical or mental challenge does not make a person inferior. Helping people with disabilities without ridiculing or patronizing them shows that you believe all people are equal, although some people need a little extra assistance. Be ready to help a disabled person by doing such things as holding open a door, carrying a package, or giving up your seat. Don't stare at disabled people or make comments about their special needs.

3 **Apologize or make up for hurting someone's feelings or causing harm.** Saying you're sorry shows that you can take responsibility for your actions and can admit when you've done something wrong. You can harm someone by what you fail to do just as easily as by what you do. Examples include breaking a promise or not sticking up for someone who is being picked on. If you hurt someone, apologize immediately and sincerely.

4 **Recognize that people of different races, religions, and backgrounds deserve to be treated the same as you expect to be treated.** Don't make jokes and rude comments about someone's skin color or beliefs. Some people have different customs; some have more money than others. It doesn't matter; all people should be treated the same.

Accepting Criticism

1 **Look at the person to show that you are paying attention.** Don't stare, make faces, or look away during the conversation. Listen carefully, and try not to be distracted. Paying attention shows courtesy; looking away shows disinterest.

2 **Say "okay."** This shows that you understand what the other person is saying. Nodding your head also shows that you understand and are still listening carefully. Use a pleasant voice. Don't mumble or be sarcastic.

3 **Don't argue.** Accepting criticism without arguing shows that you are mature. Stay calm. Try to learn from what the person is saying so you can do a better job next time. Remember that the person who is giving you criticism is only trying to help. If you disagree, wait until later to discuss the matter.

All of these skills can make your life better. Use them sincerely, and use them often. You may have to vary some of the skills to fit the situation, but give an honest effort. If you do, you will find that you will get along with others much better. You also will end up with more self-confidence than ever before.

Friendship Dos and Don'ts

Friendship is sometimes like money – it's easier to earn than it is to keep. And just like money, a friend is valuable. No friend should be misused or taken for granted.

Remember: Friendship is based on doing things and having fun together, talking with each other, and helping each other. These are the basic elements that keep friendships healthy and happy. But sometimes friends get lazy and don't show one another how much they care. When that happens, the friendship may begin to slide. The good news is friends can renew the excitement and enthusiasm they once had. All they need to do is get back to the basics.

■ Randy's Story

Randy moved to a new city in the middle of eighth grade. He was nervous, because making friends had always been difficult for him, but he was determined to try. The first week at his new school he did pretty well. He introduced himself in a confident way, was good at making conversation, and gave compliments to the other kids. They thought he seemed to be a pretty interesting guy.

Randy ran into trouble when he tried to take the relationship one step further to friendship. It seemed just when things were beginning to go well, Randy would do something that turned the other kid off. He sometimes asked very personal questions, before he knew the other kid very well. He would smother a new friend with attention: buying gifts, calling on the phone several times an evening, wanting to spend every free moment with the new friend. Randy had a lot to offer, but before the other kids had a chance to recognize what a neat person he was, he had driven them away.

Randy's story has a happy ending. When he lost a potential friend for the fourth time, he asked the other kid what he was doing wrong, and the other kid was brutally truthful with him. It hurt and embarrassed Randy, but he was smart enough, and wanted friends enough, to make changes. He now has some good friends in his new school.

Let's look at some things you should and shouldn't do in order to keep your friendships strong:

1 **Support and encourage your friends.** We all have the need to feel worthwhile. Friends help us meet that need. There are times when your friends will be down or troubled. That's the time to help them. Other times, they need to hear some encouragement and get a little push in the right direction.

If you are a friend, you hold power. You have the ability to make someone's life better. Grab it. Let your friends know that they can count on you for support.

! *There may not be a cure for every illness, but there sure is a get-well card.*

2 **Let your friends be themselves.** Even though friendships thrive on mutual interests, you and your friends won't always like everything the same way or have exactly the same interests. For example, you might like an occasional game of basketball, but it might be an absolute passion for your friend.

You and your friends shouldn't be exactly alike in the way you think, talk, act, and dress, either. You're not clones. Let your friends pursue their own interests without any interference from you (as long as those things aren't harmful, of course). Listen to them, and enjoy their excitement when they talk about things you're not familiar with.

3 Respect your friends' right to say "no." Don't try to force your friends to do something "for the sake of friendship." Never hang friendship over someone's head as an excuse to do the things you want to do. This also means you shouldn't be forced into doing something you don't want to do. Friends don't threaten to end the relationship for selfish reasons. They don't make one another feel guilty. Instead, they respect and honor one another's decisions.

! *You cannot use your friends and have them too.*

4 Don't use your friends for your own gain. Don't go to them every time you need to borrow something. Friends can give only so much before they feel they're being taken advantage of. If you do borrow something, return it as soon as you have finished using it. Friends should bring whatever they borrowed back in good condition. If not, they should offer to fix it or replace it. If you borrow money, repay it as soon as possible. Then give your friends a sincere "thank you." Make sure your friends know they can borrow things from you also. It works both ways in friendship.

! *Before borrowing money from a friend, decide which you need more.*

5 **Develop many friendships.** Remember the friendship potential we talked about earlier? There's no limit to the number of friends you should have. It's certainly okay to have a "best friend:" We all need a confidante and buddy. But be sure to branch out and get to know other people, too. Don't feel bad if you occasionally need a little time away from one another. Best friends should understand. The next time you do get together, everything will seem even better.

Include a wide variety of friends and companions in your activities; it's healthy and refreshing, and you really grow as a person. Use the skills we talked about in previous chapters to get to know more people.

6 **When a friend hurts your feelings, talk openly about why you were hurt.** Don't keep it to yourself; that just makes things worse. Negative thoughts will keep building until they suddenly come spilling out, and you say or do something that could hurt your friendship.

Be honest, and share what you're feeling, good and bad. If you hurt a friend's feelings, don't hesitate to apologize. Close friends sometimes argue and disagree with each other. That's normal. You're different people, and you shouldn't think alike. But close friends don't hold grudges; they learn to get back together quickly. Learn to talk about the problems you're having. It may be a little uncomfortable to be that honest with your feelings, but your friendship will be stronger because of it.

7 Choose friends for the right reasons. Friends should build you up, not bring you down. Don't try to be one of the "in crowd" just because you think it will make you more popular. That's just a matter of opinion, anyway.

Take some time to think about why you want to be friends with someone. Don't start changing your beliefs or doing things that you really don't enjoy or know are wrong. Friends help each other become better people. Stick with people who are good for you, who respect your feelings and care about you. Those are your real friends.

Always be yourself; then do what you know is right. The first step in any relationship is being acceptable to yourself.

▼
● *We too often love things and use people when
we should be using things and loving people.*

8 **Enjoy the uniqueness of each of your friends.** Each one is special, with special gifts and talents. Be grateful for what they can give, not annoyed by what they can't give. Don't put down their ideas and tastes just because they are different from yours; those differences are what make friendship exciting. With some friends, you may feel comfortable talking seriously; with others, you'll just go out and have fun. There will be some friends you know you can trust, and some you will be more careful with when sharing your feelings. That's fine and normal.

9 **Give constructive advice when asked (or when necessary).** When a friend needs to talk, listen without interruption. When a friend asks for advice, be honest and positive. Don't dwell on a friend's failures. Giving advice when your friend wants advice is different from constantly harping on your friend's faults. Friends won't be friends for long if one person is overly critical and bossy.

▼
● *Criticism is like lawn fertilizer – the right amount works wonders, but too much kills the grass.*

69

On the other hand, friends have faults and failings just like everyone else, and they're going to make some mistakes. There are times when you shouldn't be afraid to tell your friend to stop doing things that are morally or legally wrong, such as stealing, or things that are socially wrong, such as insulting others or starting rumors. If more people followed these guidelines for friendship, wouldn't the world be nicer for everyone?

! *It is much easier to be critical than correct.*

10 **Don't overburden your friends.** There will be times when you are angry and frustrated, and you will vent those negative feelings to a friend. That's okay. But people who constantly complain and gripe are unpleasant to be around, and their whining gets old quickly. Friends can't, and aren't supposed to, handle all your problems; they need a break sometimes. Instead of complaining, try to find a way to fix whatever is wrong. If possible, solve the problem together. If it can't be solved, let it end there. Don't continue to complain.

11 **Help your friends out of rough spots.** Many problems are hard to handle, and they can really get a person down. Your friends will get depressed or sad. So will you. Don't hesitate to offer a helping hand. Be there to listen. Be there to wipe away tears. That's very important to a friendship. In fact, many friendships become stronger and more enjoyable if you stick out the down times together.

12 **Think before you speak.** It's healthy to express your feelings instead of bottling everything up inside. Clearing the air helps a relationship grow. But beware of things that are better left unsaid. Words said in anger can cut like a knife. They can devastate a friend and, ultimately, your relationship. Think of it this way: It takes a long time to build a house, but it can be demolished in minutes. The same is true for friendship.

> *When I want to speak, let me first think: Is it kind? Is it true? Is it necessary? If not, let it be left unsaid.*

You're going to be angry with your friends sometimes, but don't let words spoken in haste ruin a valuable relationship. Don't say nasty things just because you're angry. Wait until you cool down and can sort through your feelings before you talk. You and your friends will be glad you did.

> *Always make sure your brain is in gear before you put your mouth in motion.*

Shyness

Have you ever avoided people or situations out of fear that you would make a fool of yourself? Have you ever felt so self-conscious that you wanted to run away or hide? If so, you're shy, and it's time to do something about it.

Most of us want to avoid situations in which we might fail. Maybe you've had similar feelings when you've been asked to speak in front of the class or have been singled out in a large group. A case of "stage fright" or "butterflies in the stomach" is common. Being put on the spot makes most people feel uncomfortable.

But there is a terrible feeling called shyness, which goes beyond being nervous or worried about how you will perform. Some people suffer so much from shyness that they have built an invisible prison around themselves. Their shyness makes them captives, places them in solitary confinement. They begin to think that there is no way to escape. There is. For those people, it's time to go over the wall and make a prison break.

What Is Shyness?

If you were to boil shyness down to its very bones, you would find that it's basically a fear of people. Shy people feel threatened in social situations; they lack self-confidence and are afraid of failing. Their shyness doesn't allow them to show other people their goodness.

Shyness also can be a result of poor social skills. When people don't know how to act around others, they are likely to fail. When they fail often, it's logical that they will start avoiding people. They worry about being made fun of and put down, so they flee from social situations.

Shy people have to fight their battles on the inside. They have convinced themselves that they aren't good enough. There is no doubt that they have to make some major changes in the way they think of themselves in order to defeat their feelings of inadequacy.

Shyness isn't always visible to others. Some people feel terrible inside but put on a front to hide their true feelings. In other people, shyness is obvious; they appear timid and afraid.

There are varying degrees of shyness, of course. Some people may be shy only in certain situations or with certain people. Others may be plagued with shyness all the time, regardless of where they are or whom they are with. It makes them feel and act helpless around other people. Shyness, in its worst form, is a paralyzing fear.

One thing is certain: Shyness can keep you from meeting new people and reaching your potential. Once you start to avoid other people, they, in turn, will avoid you. And no matter how hard you try, you can't keep away from everyone all the time. Most of us can't go live alone in the woods, gathering berries and honey to survive. We live in a social world. In our society, many of the good things in life revolve around interacting with others. Like the old saying goes, "You can run, but you can't hide."

◆ Maris' Story

Maris is a loner. She has no friends, eats lunch alone, and sits quietly in her classes. She is so shy that she panics when she thinks she may have to talk to someone. She keeps her eyes down in the hallways between classes, hoping no one will notice her. She feels a little more comfortable with adults, but unless a teacher or other adult talks to her first, she is usually silent with them as well.

Maris has something that none of her classmates know about – a gift for the piano and a
beautiful singing voice. She is too shy to sign up
for chorus, but she does take private music lessons.
Her teacher is trying to encourage Maris to join
the chorus and share her gift, but so far Maris
doesn't have the courage. This teacher is also trying to help Maris gain the confidence to reach out
to others her own age. She knows that Maris will
lead a lonely life if she doesn't overcome some of
her shyness. It's up to Maris to decide.

Signs of Shyness

Shy people experience many symptoms, some
physical and some emotional. The following list
contains feelings and behaviors shy people have:

- ✔ Extreme blushing
- ✔ Inability to start conversations, especially
  with strangers
- ✔ Panic attacks – sweating, dizziness, queasy
  stomach, pounding heart, dry throat
- ✔ Feeling a need to leave a situation immediately to avoid fainting, a heart attack, or
  some other disaster
- ✔ Preferring to be alone rather than taking the
  risk of being a failure around other people
- ✔ Feeling extremely self-conscious, like everyone is watching and judging

✔ Never wanting to speak up or share a personal opinion

✔ Extreme embarrassment when asked a question

✔ Avoiding people and places altogether

✔ Being unable to talk, or saying something that doesn't make sense

Doesn't sound like a lot of fun, does it? It's easy to see why shy people suffer. They lose the wonderful opportunity to share ideas and feelings with others. It's amazing how powerful shyness can be if you don't learn to overcome it.

The good news is people can learn to overcome shyness by improving social skills and self-confidence. This dynamic duo can rescue a shy person. If you are battling shyness, the social skills listed in the last chapter will help you build self-confidence. As your self-confidence grows and becomes stronger, your ability to get along with others will increase. The combination of the two is unbeatable.

Overcoming Shyness

If you frequently avoid social situations, or if your fuel tank of self-confidence is running on empty, you need to get busy. Your shy inner voice will keep telling you to do nothing, but doing nothing will change nothing, and shyness will continue to control you. Therefore, the first thing that you must do is convince yourself to change, to do something about your shyness. It will take some time, but you can do it.

> ❗ *Courage is being scared to death – and saddling up anyway.*
>
> John Wayne

Here are some tips that may help you overcome shyness:

1 Forgive yourself, and start liking yourself once again. That's the first step. None of these other tips will work until you quit criticizing yourself for past failures. They are over with, done, kaput, outta here. If you can learn from them, fine. But don't continue to beat yourself up. Tell yourself, "I am going to improve. I am going to win."

2 Play a game of H-O-R-S-E with your shyness. If you're not familiar with this idea, let me explain: In basketball, two players often play this game. One person shoots; if the shot is made, the other person tries to make the identical shot. If that player misses, he or she gets a letter from the word "horse." For example, the first time a person misses a shot the other person made, he or she gets an "H," the next miss an "O," and so on. They continue playing until one player misses five shots (spelling H-O-R-S-E). That person loses.

For your game, make a list of situations or people you have avoided in the past. Title it "Times Shyness Won." List as many examples as you can.

Now the game begins. You're going "one-on-one" with your shyness. Take any of those situations, and set a goal to beat the shy team in a game of H-O-R-S-E. Each time you accomplish one of your goals, the shy team gets a letter.

For example, if you listed, "I never raise my hand to answer a question in class," set a goal to do just that. If you raise your hand in any class, the shy team gets a letter. Continue until the shy team spells "horse."

Try to win at least one letter each day. At that rate, you could win the game in five days – an average school week. If you can do it sooner than that, great. Soon, you will get so good that you will beat the shy team at H-O-R-S-E every day. In the meantime, you are kicking the living daylights out of your shyness.

❗ *Improvement begins with "I."*

3 **Don't put yourself down.** Don't dwell on your mistakes. It's easy to pick yourself apart if you focus on negative things. If you tell yourself you're a failure, you will be. It's as simple as that. Instead, practice positive self-talk. Praise yourself when you do well. Encourage yourself; tell yourself you can succeed. Whenever negative thoughts creep into your head, stop them, and replace them with good thoughts. It really does work. Keep at it. Build yourself up instead of cutting yourself down. Concentrate on building a new, confident you.

4 **Practice conversation skills.** Think of things you are going to say before you have to say them. Imagine situations where you may be asked questions or where you'll be expected to join in, and then think about what you will say. If you're going to ask someone for help, think of how you're going to do it. Then practice, practice, practice. No one is born a conversationalist. It's a learned skill. If you want to get better at anything, you have to repeat it again and again. Practice with a friend, a brother or sister, or in front of a mirror. Pretend you're talking with a classmate; pick a topic, and have a conversation full of questions and replies. If necessary, go back to the second chapter for some specific tips on effective conversation skills.

5 **Try something new.** Begin a new hobby. Participate in a new sport or activity. Join a club you've always been interested in but didn't have the courage to join. Sing into a tape recorder. Order something from a menu that you've never tried before. What you do isn't as important as your willingness to experiment. Taking small chances builds your confidence.

Little changes in our daily routine can bring freshness and enthusiasm. Making changes helps break up the monotony and allows you to "branch out" and grow as a person. It shows that you are confident enough to take a chance. And a new, assertive you begins to develop in the process.

6 **Look in the mirror.** This may sound kind of silly, but looking at yourself and practicing eye contact and facial expressions can really help boost your assertiveness. Looking someone straight in the eye (without staring, of course) is a sign of confidence. Look at what your mouth and face look like when you say something. Say the same phrase with different voice tones and inflections. The way you say something is important. Practice a phrase until you think you've said it assertively. When you take the next step – actually saying it to somebody –you will be more comfortable.

7 **Write down your strengths.** What things do you do well? Are you allowing others to see this side of your personality? If not, pick a person, a time, and a place to use your skills and strengths. This isn't showing off; it's building your self-confidence and raising another person's opinion of you. Make it a goal to show your strengths to at least one person each day for two weeks.

8 **Begin "safe" conversations with strangers in public places.** Why strangers? Because it really doesn't matter if you fail. You may never see that person again, so you won't have to worry about the impression you make.

Decide where to begin – a grocery store, restaurant, clothing store, library. There are countless places where you can strike up a general conversation with a stranger, such as a store clerk, waiter, or librarian.

Your opening statement or question can focus on whatever is happening around you. For example, you could ask a store clerk, "Where can I find the school supplies?" or ask a waiter, "What's the special today?" Ask a librarian, "Where can I find this book?" These simple questions will make you feel more at ease when you start a conversation.

When the other person responds, see if you can keep the conversation going by asking another question or making a comment about the response, and then feel good that you had the courage to begin a conversation.

▼
● *Make up your mind you can't, and you will always be right.*

Each time you use one of these suggestions, you are making your shyness weaker and your self-confidence stronger. You should feel happy about tackling such a problem head-on.

The Time Is Now

Okay. You now have some weapons to defeat the enemy. Start preparing for battle today. Get your social skills and self-confidence in line, ready to charge. Realize that you can control what you feel and do. Rip those old negative thoughts and feelings to pieces. Destroy the prison that has held you captive.

▼
● *Nothing worthwhile is achieved without patience, hard work, and disappointments.*

Good luck in overcoming shyness and becoming more confident. You've got what it takes to be successful. Although it takes time to learn how to break away from your shyness, the only real obstacle in your way is you. Learn how to think positively. Make a plan, and set achievable goals. You're stronger than you think you are. You can do it.

You're on the road to becoming more self-confident and successful than you've ever been before. Go for it!

If you think you are beaten, you are.
If you think you dare not, you don't.
If you like to win, but you think you can't,
It is almost certain you won't.
If you think you'll lose, you've lost,
For out of the world we find
Success begins with a fellow's will –
It's all in the state of mind.
If you think you are outclassed, you are,
You've got to think high to rise,
You've got to be sure of yourself before
You can ever win a prize.
Life's battles don't always go
To the stronger or faster man,
But sooner or later the man who wins
Is the man WHO THINKS HE CAN!